D1397572

The WorLD's DeaDLiEsT NATURAL DISASTERS

Claire Henry

PowerKiDS press

New York

Published in 2014 by The Rosen Publishing Group, Inc.
29 East 21st Street, New York, NY 10010

First Edition

Produced for Rosen by Cyan Candy, LLC
Editor: Joshua Shadowens
Designer: Erica Clendening, Cyan Candy

Photo Credits: Cover and p. 12 NigelSpiers / Shutterstock.com, pp. 4, 5, 11, 20 Shuterstock.
com; p. 8 MISHELLA / Shutterstock.com; p. 9 John Huntington / Shutterstock.com; p. 10 NASA
image by Jeff Schmaltz, MODIS Land Rapid Response Team, Goddard Space Flight Center, via
Wikimedia Commons; pp. 13 (top, middle, bottom), 17, 19 (top, bottom), 20, 22, 23 (top, bottom)
Wikimedia Commons; pp. 14, 15 arindambanerjee / Shutterstock.com; p. 16 Paul Prescott /
Shutterstock.com; p. 18 Underwood & Underwood @ 1906, via Wikimedia Commons; p. 21
KOMUnews, via Wikimedia Commons; p. 24 Suizaperuana, via Wikimedia Commons; p. 25 Morn
the Gorn, via Wikimedia Commons; p. 26 DanHobley, via Wikimedia Commons; p. 30 Terry
Poche / Shutterstock.com.

Library of Congress Cataloging-in-Publication Data

Henry, Claire, 1975–
 The world's deadliest natural disasters / by Claire Henry. — First edition.
     pages cm. — (The world's deadliest)
 Includes index.
 ISBN 978-1-4777-6142-7 (library binding) — ISBN 978-1-4777-6147-2 (pbk.) —
 ISBN 978-1-4777-6148-9 (6-pack)
 1. Natural disasters—Juvenile literature. I. Title.
 GB5019.H46 2014
 363.34'92—dc23
                            2013020346

Manufactured in the United States of America

CPSIA Compliance Information: Batch #W14PK8: For Further Information contact Rosen Publishing, New York, New York at 1-800-237-9932

TABLE OF CONTENTS

NATURE TURNS DEADLY

On the morning of December 26, 2004, a massive earthquake shook the land below the Indian Ocean. As the people of Indonesia, Thailand, and other coastal countries woke, they had no idea that a tsunami, or series of giant waves of water, was racing toward them. Minutes after the earthquake, waves as high as 100 feet (30 m) began crashing onto the land. By day's end, over 220,000 people had been killed, and millions more had lost their homes.

TSUNAMI WAVE

The damage after the 2004 Indian Ocean tsunami was devastating. Here are ruined homes in Galle, Sri Lanka, one of the many places affected by this disaster.

The Indian Ocean tsunami was one of the worst natural disasters ever recorded. However, Earth's history is filled with destructive natural events, including hurricanes, **tornadoes**, and volcanic eruptions. Some of these natural disasters have even wiped out entire cities!

Every year, natural disasters cause death and injuries all over the world. They can also cause damage to buildings, roads, and natural features such as forests and oceans. Some types of natural disasters can be predicted days, or even weeks, before they strike.

DEADLIEST NATURAL

NAME	DATE
Haiti Earthquake	January 12, 2010
Indian Ocean Earthquake and Tsunami	December 16, 2004
Cyclone Nargis	May 2, 2008
Kashmir Earthquake	October 8, 2005
Sichuan Earthquake	May 12, 2008
European Heat Wave	June–August 2003
Russian Heat Wave and Wildfires	July–September 2010
Bam Earthquake	May 26, 2003
Japanese Earthquake and Tsunami	March 11, 2011
Bhuj Earthquake	January 26, 2001

Other types of disasters, though, can occur with almost no warning. In this book you will read about some of the deadliest natural disasters in history. Prepare to witness the fierce and violent power of nature!

DISASTERS 2000–2012

LOCATION	STRENGTH	DEATH TOLL
Haiti	7.0 magnitude	316,000
Indian Ocean's surrounding countries	9.0–9.3 magnitude	220,000
Myanmar	category 4	138,366
Pakistan	7.6 magnitude	100,000
China	8.0 magnitude	87,587
Western Europe	high temperature of 118°F (48°C)	70,000
Russia	temperature of 111°F (44°C)	55,790
Iran	6.6 magnitude	31,000
Japan	9.0 magnitude	20,896
India	7.7 magnitude	20,023

TROPICAL CYCLONES: STORMS UNDER PRESSURE

A **tropical cyclone** is a powerful storm with strong winds and heavy rain. These storms form over warm, tropical waters near the Earth's **equator**. They use the warm waters below as energy, growing in strength as they move over large distances. As a tropical cyclone moves, its winds swirl around an area of low pressure called the eye of the storm.

Tropical cyclones that form in the Atlantic Ocean and eastern Pacific Ocean are called hurricanes. Tropical cyclones that form in the northwestern Pacific, near Asia, are called typhoons. Storms in the South Pacific and Indian oceans are called cyclones.

During Hurricane Sandy, many homes and cars, such as this one in New

HURRICANE SANDY

In October 2012, Hurricane Sandy traveled through the Caribbean and up the east coast of the United States. Over 200 people were killed across seven countries. Homes and businesses, many in New York and New Jersey, were destroyed by flooding and fires. In the United States alone, Hurricane Sandy caused about $75 billion in damage.

THE GREAT HURRICANE OF 1780

The deadliest Atlantic hurricane ever recorded struck islands in the Caribbean Sea in October 1780. About 22,000 people died. The hurricane occurred during the American Revolution, and many British and French ships were lost.

BHOLA CYCLONE

This powerful storm, the deadliest tropical cyclone ever recorded, made landfall in Bangladesh on November 11, 1970. Between 300,000 and 500,000 people were killed. The rising ocean water, called a **storm surge**, destroyed entire villages.

HURRICANE KATRINA

Hurricane Katrina hit Louisiana and other Gulf Coast states on August 29, 2005. In New Orleans a system of **levees**, or

CYCLONE

Many major roads into and out of New Orleans were damaged by Hurricane Katrina.

structures built to prevent flooding, failed. Waters rose and flooded 80 percent of the city. At least 1,836 people in seven states were killed and thousands more lost their homes.

GALVESTON HURRICANE OF 1900

This hurricane struck Galveston Island, Texas, on September 8, 1900. About 8,000 people were killed, making the Galveston Hurricane the deadliest natural disaster in US history.

EARTHQUAKES: SHIFTS AND SHAKES

The Earth's **crust**, or outer layer, is made up of many pieces, called **plates**. These plates are moving, very slowly, in different directions. Sometimes they slide against, or even bump into each other. When this happens, we feel the ground beneath us shake. This is called an earthquake.

Earthquakes are caused by shifts in the **tectonic** plates of the Earth. When a major earthquake strikes, it can rip bridges and roads apart.

CHILE TSUNAMI 1960

LEAST INTENSE

MOST INTENSE

Some earthquakes are so small that we do not even feel them. Others, though, are strong enough to bring down buildings. The size, or strength, of an earthquake is called the **magnitude**. The largest earthquake on record occurred in Chile, in South America, in 1960. It had a magnitude of 9.5 and left about 2 million people without homes!

Above: The 1960 Chilean tsunami affected the entire Pacific Basin, including Hilo, Hawaii.

Right: A lone man walks

SHAANXI EARTHQUAKE OF 1556

The deadliest earthquake in history occurred in China's Shaanxi province on January 23, 1556. At the time, most people in the area lived in manmade caves carved into cliffs. The giant earthquake caused **landslides**, which destroyed the cliffs. About 830,000 people were killed.

TANGSHAN EARTHQUAKE

This earthquake, the deadliest of the twentieth century, shook the city of Tangshan, in China, on July 28, 1976. Though the earthquake lasted only about 15 seconds, 85 percent of the city's buildings were destroyed. Some estimates say about 255,000 people died, though that number could be as high as 655,000.

These children attend school in Cité Soleil, a poor neighborhood in the Haitian capital of Port-au-Prince. It took almost two weeks for help to get to Cité Soleil after the hurricane.

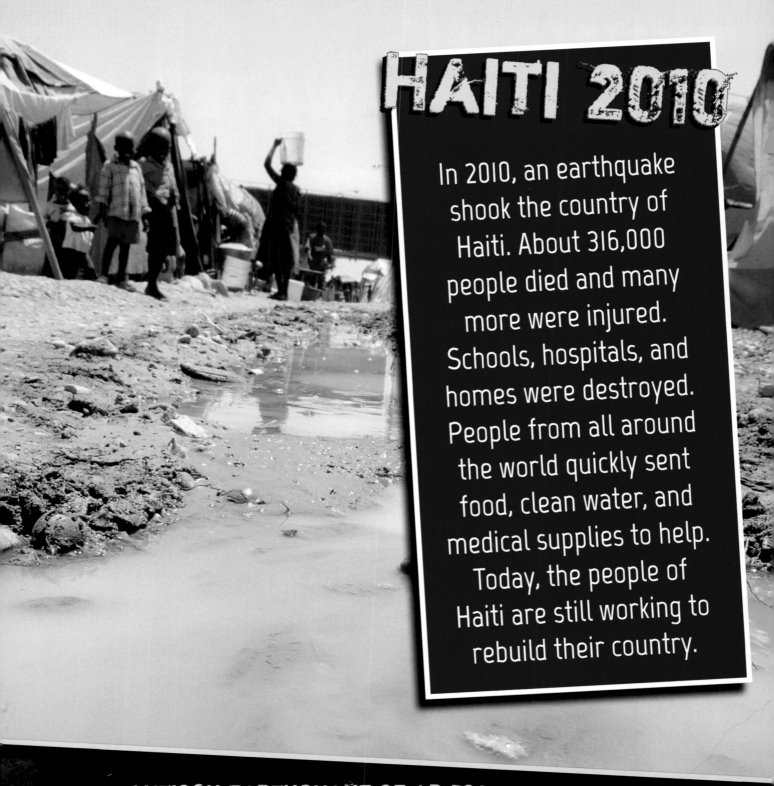

HAITI 2010

In 2010, an earthquake shook the country of Haiti. About 316,000 people died and many more were injured. Schools, hospitals, and homes were destroyed. People from all around the world quickly sent food, clean water, and medical supplies to help. Today, the people of Haiti are still working to rebuild their country.

ANTIOCH EARTHQUAKE OF AD 526

In late May, in the year AD 526, an earthquake shook the ancient city of Antioch, which is now part of Turkey. Many buildings were damaged by the earthquake itself, and many more were destroyed by a massive fire. About 250,000 people were killed.

TSUNAMIS: WALLS OF WATER

When earthquakes occur in areas near people, they can bring down buildings and cause injuries and deaths. Earthquakes can actually cause damage, though, even when they occur hundreds of miles (km) from the nearest humans.

About 70 percent of Earth is covered by water. When Earth's plates shift and move under an ocean, large amounts of ocean water are moved, too. That water spreads outward, in waves, from the area of the earthquake. This series of waves, called

In 2004, a giant tsunami hit the countries surrounding the Indian Ocean. Here, onlookers view the aftermath of the storm. A car is in a riverbank in Khao Lak, Thailand.

a tsunami, grows bigger and more powerful as it moves toward land. As the waves crash onto the shore, they can sweep away everything in their path!

JAPANESE EARTHQUAKE AND TSUNAMI

On March 11, 2011, an earthquake occurred off the coast of Japan. Just minutes later, waves as high as 124 feet (38 m) swept over Japan's coast. About 28,700 people were killed. The tsunami also flooded and damaged the Fukushima Daiichi nuclear power plant, releasing dangerous **radioactive** energy into the air.

This helicopter is delivering food to survivors in the city of Sendai. Sendai is the largest city in Tohoku and, before the tsunami, had a population of over a million people.

MESSINA EARTHQUAKE AND TSUNAMI

On December 28, 1908, an earthquake occurred in the city Messina, on the island of Sicily, which is part of Italy. A tsuna waves as high as 39 feet (12 m) rushed toward Sicily and mai Italy. Between 100,000 and 200,000 people were killed.

LISBON EARTHQUAKE AND TSUNAMI OF 1755

The Lisbon Earthquake occurred in the Atlantic Ocean, near Portugal. About 40 minutes after the earthquake, a tsunami c into Lisbon, destroying the harbor, homes, and even fortresse along the coast.

MESSINA, 1908

About 50,000 people died. Lisbon's royal library and many important documents and works of art were lost.

ARICA EARTHQUAKE AND TSUNAMI

A powerful earthquake occurred off the coast of Peru on August 16, 1868. The earthquake caused a tsunami that traveled across the Pacific Ocean, pushing waves onshore in South America, Hawaii, Japan, and New Zealand. About 70,000 people were killed.

TORNADOES: TWISTING TERROR

A tornado is a storm with funnel-shaped clouds that produce strong, spinning winds. Tornadoes form during thunderstorms when warm, moist air rises and cools. Clouds form, and as the warm air cools, it releases heat. This heat is energy for the thunderstorm. As more warm air moves up toward the clouds, the funnel of the tornado forms.

Inside the funnel, winds can swirl as fast as 300 miles per hour (483 km/h). Tornadoes often occur in groups. They can travel at a speed of 40 miles per hour (64 km/h) and destroy anything they touch.

TORNADO

JOPLIN TORNADO

On May 22, 2011, a powerful tornado moved through the town of Joplin, Missouri. The tornado, with a funnel almost 1 mile (1.6 km) wide, destroyed entire neighborhoods in its path. Over 1,000 people were injured and 158 were killed, making this tornado the deadliest in the United States in more than 60 years.

The tornado that hit Joplin was an EF5 on the Enhanced Fujita Scale, which rates the strength of tornadoes based on the damage they cause. An EF5 is the highest rating on the scale.

DAULATPUR-SATURIA TORNADO

The deadliest tornado on record occurred in Bangladesh on April 26, 1989. About 1,300 people were killed, and 12,000 more were injured. In some areas every building was leveled, and 80,000 people were left without homes.

TRI-STATE TORNADO

The Tri-State Tornado, named because it traveled a path through three states, is the deadliest tornado in US history. On March 18, 1925, it moved through Missouri, Illinois, and Indiana, lasting for over three hours. The tornado killed 695 people and injured thousands more.

This photo shows the damage and destruction in the town of Griffin, Indiana, after the Tri-State Tornado.

Left: This map shows all the tornado warnings (red), thunderstorm warnings (yellow), and flood warnings (green) in the southeastern United States on April 27, 2011.
Below: This map shows the rainfall, in inches, from April 22, 2011, to April 29, 2011. Scientists use maps like these to predict where tornadoes will occur.

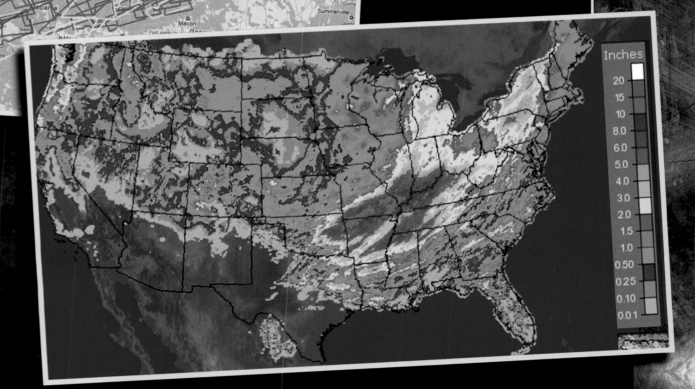

Inches
20
15
10
8.0
6.0
5.0
4.0
3.0
2.0
1.5
1.0
0.50
0.25
0.10
0.01

VALETTA, MALTA TORNADO

Some records say this tornado occurred in 1551, while others say it was 1556. We do know that it killed about 600 people. The tornado began over water and moved through the island of Malta's Grand Harbour, where it destroyed an entire fleet of warships.

MORE EXTREME WEATHER

HUASCARÁN AVALANCHE

An avalanche is a large amount of snow, ice, earth, or rock that slides down a mountain. On May 31, 1970, an earthquake occurred off the coast of Peru. The earthquake caused a massive avalanche on Huascarán Mountain. The mass of snow, ice, and rock moved down the mountain at about 300 miles per hour (483 km/h), burying towns and killing 20,000 people.

This is Mount Huascarán as it appears today. The southern summit of the mountain is the highest point in Peru.

This is the view of Vesuvius from Pompeii. Today, Pompeii is a tourist destination, attracting nearly 3 million visitors per year.

MOUNT VESUVIUS ERUPTION OF AD 79

Vesuvius is a 4,190-foot-(1,277 m) tall volcano in Italy. In the year AD 79, Vesuvius **erupted**, spewing volcanic ash, rocks, and deadly gases 20.5 miles (33 km) into the air. About 16,000 people died during the eruption. The ancient cities of Pompeii and Herculaneum were completely buried by ash and were forgotten about for hundreds of years!

VENEZUELA RAINS AND MUDSLIDES

Over three days in 1999, 36 inches (91 cm) of rain fell on Venezuela's northern coast. That is as much rain as the area usually gets in an entire year! The heavy rain caused many shallow landslides. On December 15, huge amounts of mud and **debris** flowed toward the ocean, swallowing entire towns. About 15,000 people were killed, though many of the bodies were swept out to sea or buried in mud, never to be found.

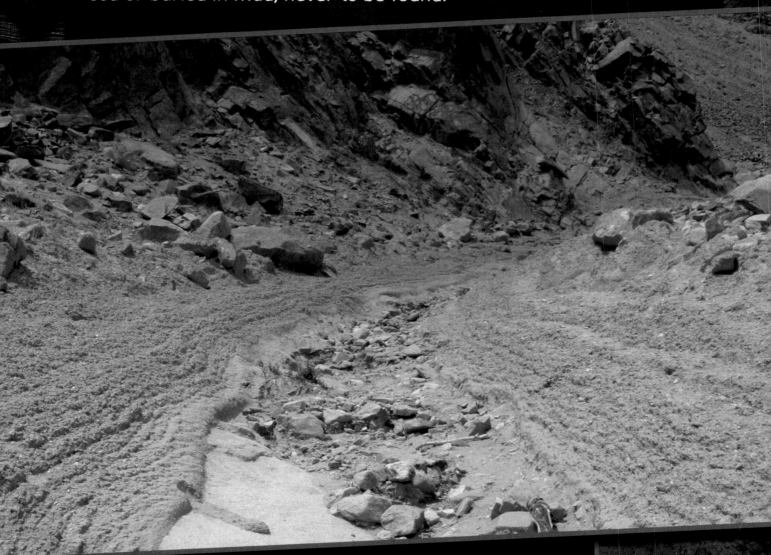

This photo shows a mud and debris path in the Ladakh region of India. The flooding and mudslides were caused by heavy storms in August 2010.

NATURAL DISASTERS AROUND THE WORLD

17 2
25 26 8
13 20 10 9
15 12 18 24 11
6 5 27 23
16
3 7 28 4 22
21 1
19
14

1. Indian Ocean Tsunami-
   Indian Ocean, Indonesia
2. Hurricane Sandy-
   New York/New Jersey
3. Great Hurricane of 1780-
   Caribbean Sea
4. Bhola Cyclone- Bangladesh
5. Hurricane Katrina-
   New Orleans
6. Galveston Hurricane-
   Galveston, Texas
7. Haiti Earthquake- Haiti
8. Shaanxi Earthquake-
   China (Shaanxi Province)
9. Tangshan Earthquake-
   Tangshan, China
10. Antioch Earthquake-

11. Japanese Tsunami- Japan
12. Messina Earthquake-
    Messina, Sicily, Italy
13. Lisbon Earthquake-
    Lisbon, Portugal
14. Arica Earthquake- Arica
    (was in Peru, now in Chile)
15. Joplin Tornado-Joplin,
    Missouri
16. Daulatpur-Saturia
    Tornado- Bangladesh
17. Tri-State Tornado-
    Missouri/Illinois/Indiana
18. Valetta, Malta
    Tornado- Malta
19. Huascarán Avalanche-
    Peru

20. Mount Vesuvius
    Eruption- Italy
21. Venezuela Rains and
    Mudslides- Venezuela
22. Cyclone Nargis- Myanmar
23. Kashmir Earthquake-
    Pakistan
24. Sichuan Earthquake-
    China
25. European Heat Wave-
    Western Europe (France)
26. Russian Heat Wave-
    Russia
27. Bam Earthquake- Iran
28. Bhuj Earthquake-India

DEADLIEST DISASTERS

Here is a list of the deadliest natural disasters in human history. Some are very recent, while others occurred hundreds of years ago. You will find descriptions of many of these disasters in the pages of this book. You can read more about the other events on the list in books, newspaper articles, and on the Internet.

DEADLIEST NATURAL DISASTERS

NAME	DATE
China Floods of 1931	July–August 1931
1887 Yellow River Floods	September 1887
Shaanxi Earthquake	January 23, 1556
Tangshan Earthquake	July 28, 1976
Bhola Cyclone	November 11, 1970
Haiti Earthquake	January 12, 2010
1839 India Cyclone	November 25, 1839
1737 Calcutta Cyclone	October 7, 1737
Antioch Earthquake of 526	May 526
Haiyuan Earthquake	December 16, 1920

CHINA FLOODS OF 1931

In 1930, central China was nearing the end of a long drought, or period with little or no rain. That winter, there were many heavy snowstorms. As the snow melted in the spring, heavy rains came as well, raising water levels in rivers and lakes. In the summer of 1931, the Yangtze and Huai rivers flooded, killing millions of people. Even more died from diseases spread by contaminated water.

IN HUMAN HISTORY

LOCATION	DEATH TOLL
Central China	2,500,000–3,700,000
Northern China	900,000–2,000,000
Shaanxi Province, China	830,000
Tangshan, China	250,000–779,000
Bangladesh	500,000
Haiti	316,000
Coringa, Andhra Pradesh, India	300,000
Calcutta, India	300,000
Turkey	250,000
Haiyuan County, Ningxia Huizu, China	235,5000

Note—It is not always possible to know the exact number of people killed in a natural disaster. Some events occurred before precise records were kept. Sometimes the bodies of victims are simply never found. In this book, we have made every effort to use the most reliable numbers available.

PREDICTING NATURE

Throughout history, natural disasters have had a deadly effect on humans. They have played a huge part in where and how people live. Today, all across the world, scientists are working to understand more about what causes natural disasters and how they work. The more they learn, the better they can predict when and where natural disasters will occur. An early warning may give people a chance to escape before nature strikes!

This helicopter carries sandbags to help plug a broken levee after Hurricane Katrina hit New Orleans.

GLOSSARY

avalanche (A-vuh-lanch) When a large amount of snow, ice, earth, or dirt slides down a mountainside.

crust (KRUST) The outer, or top, layer of a planet.

debris (duh-BREE) The remains of something broken down or destroyed.

drought (DROWT) A period of dryness that causes harm to crops.

equator (ih-KWAY-tur) The imaginary line around Earth that separates it into two parts, northern and southern.

erupted (ih-RUP-ted) To have had a volcano send up gases, smoke, or lava.

landslides (LAND-slydz) The movements of rock or earth down slopes.

levees (LEH-veez) Raised riverbanks used to stop a river from overflowing.

magnitude (MAG-nih-tood) The measurement of something's strength.

plates (PLAYTS) The moving pieces of Earth's crust, the top layer of Earth.

predicted (prih-DIKT-ed) To make a guess based on facts or knowledge.

radioactive (ray-dee-oh-AK-tiv) Giving off rays of light, heat, or energy.

storm surge (STORM SURJ) When storms make the sea level rise.

tornadoes (tawr-NAY-dohs) Storms with a funnel-shaped cloud that produce strong, spinning winds.

tropical cyclone (TRAH-puh-kul SY-klohn) A storm with strong, spinning winds.

tsunami (soo-NAH-mee) A series of waves caused by a movement in Earth's crust on the ocean floor.

INDEX

WEBSITES

Due to the changing nature of Internet links, PowerKids Press has developed
an online list of websites related to the subject of this book. This site is updated
regularly. Please use this link to access the list:
www.powerkids.com/twd/natur/